I Want to Teach my CHiLD About Values

BY

MARCY W. BRYAN

Standard

I Want to Teach My Child About Values
© 2005 Standard Publishing, Cincinnati,
Ohio. A division of Standex International
Corporation. All rights reserved. Printed
in China.

Produced by Susan Lingo Books™
Cover and interior by Diana Walters

12 11 10 09 08 07 06 05   9 8 7 6 5 4 3 2 1
0-7847-1763-X

Contents

Introduction

Why teach your child about values?

Values make up the framework for most of our actions. Qualities such as honesty, love, and optimism are sometimes hard to evaluate in ourselves, but they deeply affect how we deal with our friends, our enemies, and, most importantly, our children. This book was written to encourage you. It's full of things to think about and ideas to try. But please don't stop with what you find here. God might bring you other, perhaps more creative, ways to strengthen you as you guide your children toward an understanding of godly values.

As you learn, write your ideas down. Make a notebook. Pass them on. It's my sincere hope that this little book will help you and your children not only make "value-growing" part of your daily experience but also help you grow together as a family and be drawn even closer to God. Ultimately, a family that truly practices values together will polish each other to a sparkly shine, reflecting our Savior and thus attracting the world.

Marcy W. Bryan

Where Do You Stand?

Working toward helping your child learn about values and how they affect his life is an important part of parenting. The following questionnaire will help you evaluate your own strengths and weaknesses and where your beliefs and philosophies fit in. Circle the box with the number that best corresponds to your answer. Then add up the total of your answers and check out the How You Scored box! (Retake the quiz after reading the book to see if your score changed!)

OPTIONS

❶ Strongly agree

❷ Agree somewhat

❸ Disagree somewhat

❹ Strongly disagree

I REGULARLY RETURN MY SHOPPING CART INSTEAD OF LEAVING IT BESIDE MY CAR.

❶ ❷ ❸ ❹

I HOLD DOORS OPEN TO STORES, MALLS, OR RESTAURANTS FOR PEOPLE COMING IN AFTER ME.

❶ ❷ ❸ ❹

I GIVE MONEY (OR OTHER TYPES OF HELP) TO NEEDY PEOPLE I SEE.

❶ ❷ ❸ ❹

I TRULY LISTEN TO WHAT PEOPLE ARE SAYING TO ME INSTEAD OF "ZONING OUT."

❶ ❷ ❸ ❹

I KNOW ALL MY NEIGHBORS BY NAME AND CHECK ON THE OLDER ONES.

❶ ❷ ❸ ❹

I NEVER TAKE OFFICE SUPPLIES FROM WORK TO USE AT HOME FOR PERSONAL THINGS.

❶ ❷ ❸ ❹

I OBEY EVERY TRAFFIC SIGN AND ALWAYS DRIVE THE SPEED LIMIT.

❶ ❷ ❸ ❹

I KEEP UP ON WORLD EVENTS AND REGULARLY GIVE TO PEOPLE IN NEED AROUND THE WORLD.

❶ ❷ ❸ ❹

I DON'T PICK ON MY CHILDREN OR TEASE THEM TO THE POINT OF FRUSTRATION.

❶ ❷ ❸ ❹

I PICK UP THE TRASH I SEE WHILE ON WALKS AND PUT IT IN THE PROPER RECEPTACLE.

❶ ❷ ❸ ❹

HOW YOU SCORED

32—40 Give yourself a pat on the back! You care for others, you nurture your children, and you are a good steward of God's earth. The habits you've worked so hard to adopt are the ones your children are watching on a daily basis, and they have a good chance of acquiring them as well!

21—31 Your values might need a little polishing to really shine! As you work on embedding more positive values, help your child realize that values are to be learned and exercised throughout his life—and that God isn't done with him yet as you work on each area as a family!

10—20 Values are something you may struggle with. You may not have had many positive role models as a child or you just didn't realize that your behavior was important. But it's never too late to "sow the seeds of virtues" into your life. Work on each value together with your child as you grow closer as a family.

What Is a Value and Is It Contagious?

Val·ue (val'-yoo) n. An ideal, attitude, belief, custom, or institution that affects the way people behave toward each other and their surroundings. Values are typically considered good. Bad values are called "vices."

You say virtue, I say value.

Values, once forgotten in our self-centered culture of super-egos and "me," have resurfaced—and none too soon!

Values are in vogue—finally!

key point

VALUES ARE THE FRAME-WORK FOR A WELL-LIVED LIFE.

The idea of living with virtues is as old as the Garden of Eden … and the fall. The ancient Greek philosophers Socrates and Plato created a list of virtues, and later Christianity offered its own official list, including faith, hope, and charity. Virtues, or values, when understood and practiced, build a better person.

Teaching values was a common practice in homes, schools, and churches during the early years of our country. Then came the 1960s, when "old things" became "uncool." After several decades of sex, drugs, rock and roll, and materialism, we've returned to values to keep from losing any remnant of moral fiber that might be left. Values are back.

Since values are learned by modeling, whoever or whatever spends the most time with our kids will teach them values. This means that television, friends, movies, school, and books have the potential to exert more influence than we do. To teach our children God-centered values, we must model values for them.

Read Colossians 3:12-17 to see how we're to "clothe ourselves," then discuss the following:

• What are we to clothe ourselves with?

• What happens when we value others and treat them with kindness?

• How does clothing ourselves with these qualities draw us closer to God?

• What binds our virtues in perfect unity?

BIG BIBLE POINT

The King James Version is one of the few translations to use the word "virtue."

• In Old Testament Hebrew, the word "virtue" meant a force, like a powerful army.

• In the Gospels, "virtue" meant the "miraculous (healing) powers" of Christ.

• To Paul, the word "virtue" meant "manliness or valor"—a quality that makes someone stand out above the crowd.

96 percent of parents with kids under 13 say that they have the primary responsibility for teaching their children values.

(The Barna Group, 2003)

What makes you value-able?

A piece of gold doesn't decide it is valuable. People have decided that gold is pretty and rare and therefore worthy to be desired and searched for. Like gold, you have value—and thus the ability to develop the right values—because someone outside of you said so.

You are God's precious child.

The One who formed you, who watches over you, who came to save you, and who died for you *should* get to say how much you are worth, right? Jesus calls us "friends." We are valuable because God says so. Sadly, we do not always believe it, and that makes it hard to plant that idea deep into our children's hearts.

GOD CREATED THE WORLD—AND EACH OF US. AND HE SAW THAT IT WAS GOOD!

TIPS FOR 'TWEENS

- Thank God for your children in front of them.

- Watch your kids' favorite TV show or movie with them. Help them evaluate the values they see and hear from the media.

- Ask what their church friends like. Does your 'tween feel valued at church?

- What do they like or dislike about school or neighborhood friends?

Try to imagine with your child God's perspective concerning his creation. For example, you might ask your child what it means when God says, "I will never leave nor forsake you"(Joshua 1:5). If God didn't care for us, would He stay beside us always? Surrounding your family with Scripture can help overwrite the lies Satan tells your kids about their worth to God.

TIPS FOR TODDLERS

Tape a photo of your toddler on a craft stick and ask, "Who made you beautiful?" Have your child hold up the stick and say, "God did!" Ask, "Where did He make you beautiful?" Have your child trace a large circle with the picture stick and say, "Inside and out!"

Read and learn Scriptures that suggest the value God places on human beings (start with verses from Psalm 139). Make a list with your kids of how God sees us and why. It might surprise you. Make a conscious effort to help your children view themselves through God's eyes. It's never too early to start!

Tell your children stories about your own childhood and their family heritage. I always remember my mother saying, "Robinsons keep their word!" Each time she said it, she reemphasized the fact that I was a Robinson and must keep my word. We're part of our earthly families, but we're part of God's heavenly family as well. Remind your kids of their special identities often!

key point
GOD MADE YOU BEAUTIFUL, INSIDE AND OUT.

key point
GOD STAYS WITH US BECAUSE HE LOVES US.

TRY THIS!

Share these verses with your child, then ask: "If God didn't value you so greatly, would He save (or help, and so on) you?"

• *God will save us (Jeremiah 30:10).*
• *God will help us (Isaiah 41:10).*
• *God will make us strong (Isaiah 45:5).*
• *God will give us wisdom (1 Kings 3:12).*
• *God has called us by name (Isaiah 43:1).*

Guard God's precious gifts!

key point
OUR VALUE AND IDENTITY ARE IN JESUS!

Satan is the sworn enemy of God. Beaten by God and tossed out of heaven, he wants revenge. But since God is untouchable and Jesus conquered him at the resurrection, who or what can be his next target? What is precious enough to steal and thus cause God pain? *You are.* It's nothing personal. Satan might not hate you directly, but he despises your Father (God).

So how does the enemy attack us? According to Scripture, like a thief he tries to sneak in and steal our joy and our love for God, family, and friends. If he can make us believe even a tiny lie, he begins to draw us, one inch at a time, away from the Truth. All he said to Eve was, "You will not surely die" (Genesis 3:4). And, although Eve didn't drop dead on the spot, physical and spiritual death came to humanity through this one "little" lie. It ultimately cost God His Son.

key point
CONTINUALLY SEEK GOD'S TRUTH.

CONSIDER THIS …

- How do you tell your child you value him or her?
- Do you criticize more than compliment your child?
- Are you your child's "cheer-leader" and advocate?
- Are you a "safe zone" for your child to come to anytime?

Once lies get into our children's minds, they are very hard to get out. Glamour magazines encourage us to be unhappy with the bodies God gave us. Television shows say it's cool to disrespect parents. Songs suggest that hurting people is fun. Movies say that using others for our own pleasure is okay to get our needs met. Satan is the king of liars: when you believe one of his lies, you hurt yourself.

Too many kids base their self-worth on media messages!

KIDS SPEND AS MUCH TIME WITH TV, COMPUTERS, AND OTHER MEDIA DAILY AS THEY DO IN THE CLASSROOM.

61% OF KIDS LIVE IN HOMES WITH NO RULES REGARDING TV USAGE.

THE AVERAGE CHILD SEES NEARLY 350,000 ADS BY THE TIME HE REACHES HIGH SCHOOL.

BY SIXTH GRADE, MOST KIDS HAVE SEEN 8,000 MURDERS AND 100,000 OTHER ACTS OF VIOLENCE ON TV AND IN MOVIES.

How can we fight back? Pray for God to show our children where lies come from. Be aware of what your children see and hear. Talk with them about positive and negative media messages. Hold a contest to see who can memorize the most Scripture. And help your child nurture the truth that God made him, that his true value is in Jesus, and that he is loved and valued!

Values are learned, then lived.

Everything we do and say reflects our values, from what we think about others to how we perceive ourselves. Our values often "speak" louder than words. What messages are you sending?

Be courageous.

September 11, 2001, gave us many examples of extraordinary courage, bravery, and valor. But courage can be found closer to home: the single mom studying for her GED or the neighbor with cancer who smiles through the pain. All of these people are equally courageous.

Courage is action in the face of fear. John Wayne once said, "Courage is being scared to death but saddling up anyway." Sadly, fear rather than courage captures many people. "What-ifs" rule our days and haunt our nights. Fear of failure can imprison us and our children. What can we do to help our kids find courage in their lives?

"Courage is the ladder on which all other virtues mount."
— Clara Booth Luce

TARGET MOMENT
When you are afraid, try these simple steps:

1. Tell someone you love.
2. Hold hands and pray.
3. Trust God!
4. Step ahead; take action.
5. Thank God for helping you be brave.

First of all, ask God to help your children overcome their feelings of fear and to use that force for good. Encourage them to feel the fear (don't deny it, or it will just grow), then face their fears and accept the challenge. Encourage them to try out for the school play, join a soccer team, or even try skating. But make sure you give them the grace to try and fail. Unconditional love is one of the greatest weapons against fear.

Have each family member describe something she has never done before and might like to try. Take turns helping each person try something new. Experiencing new interests as a family will make it easier for each person to step out bravely!

key point
BRAVERY IS OFTEN BORN OF FEAR.

key point
TRUSTING GOD GIVES US COURAGE.

The bottom line is that fear boils down to a lack of trust. The more your child learns to trust God and His will, the braver your child will become. Pray for him to know God intimately and to see God in his life daily. Courage is bound to follow.

"Twenty years from now you will be more disappointed by the things you didn't do than by the ones you did. So throw off the bowlines. Sail away from the safe harbor. Catch the trade winds in your sails. Explore. Dream. Discover."
—Mark Twain

VALUES ARE LEARNED, THEN LIVED.

Be faithful.

Belief is a powerful thing. Research teams have found that "religiously active" people live considerably longer than the nonreligious. Interestingly, the lack of religious involvement has the equivalent effect on a person's lifespan as smoking one pack of cigarettes a day for forty years.

key point

FAITH DRAWS US TO GOD.

LIVING BY FAITH IS THE BEST RULE OF THUMB!

How do you help your kids believe in God? First, let them know that God is real to you. Often our kids struggle with faith because we do. Hebrews 11:1 tells us that "faith is being sure of what we hope for and certain of what we do not see." Tell your children that you have faith that God loves and cares for us. Show them evidence in His word, in His nature, and in your own loving family. Pray with your children that they acknowledge God as the giver of all good things.

Knowing God is in control

Lower stress

FAITH

Better life

A positive outlook

Talk to your kids about your relationship with God. Sometimes we only show the more positive parts of our spiritual journey, but we must show our struggles as well. This is the stuff of which faith is built. And faith building often doesn't feel good at the time. Hebrews 12:11 reminds us that when we have faith through tough times, we're rewarded with grace!

FAITH MAKES THE RIDE THROUGH LIFE SMOOTHER!

Encourage your kids to have faith. Remind them what it was like to learn to ride a bike—when just looking at that big contraption was scary! Eventually they chose to get on and try it out—and didn't give up after the first or even second fall! That's the biggest step of faith: *choosing it.* It's scary, yes. But the "ride" is so worth it!

key point
CHOOSE AND USE YOUR FAITH!

A PRAYER OF FAITH

Say this prayer together out loud. Add tapping rhythms if you desire.

God, I believe in you.
God, I believe you are who you say you are.
   (List some of God's attributes.)
God, I believe you will do what you say you will do.
   (Name some of God's promises.)
God, I believe I am who you say I am.
   (List some examples, such as "I'm precious in your sight; I'm the apple of your eye; I'm your child.")

   (Adapted from *Believing God*, by Beth Moore)

Be thankful.

Do you nag your kids to say please and thank you? Does gratefulness seem to be in short supply? How about *you*? Do you say thank you to the fast-food clerk, the checkout lady, or the police officer writing you a ticket—or to your children? (Okay, I didn't thank the officer, either.)

key point
BE GRATEFUL IN ALL THINGS!

"There are only two ways to live your life. One is as though nothing is a miracle. The other is as though everything is a miracle."
—Albert Einstein

key point
LOOK FOR GOD'S KINDNESS IN THE WORLD.

Thank-you notes are the "push-ups" of gratefulness.

• **Set aside one day for thank-yous.**

• **Kids can draw thank-you pictures.**

• **Make templates on the computer and let the kids "fill in the blanks" for fun thank-you notes.**

• **Call relatives to express your love and thanks.**

My young daughter Megh wanted to check out a book from the library "by herself." When she was handed the book, I said, "Say 'Thank you, ma'am.'" Megh looked up at me and said, "But you didn't." Ouch! She was right. We teach our children to be thankful by being grateful for small things ourselves.

Thanking one another says, "I love you!"

Remembering to be thankful isn't always easy. But Ephesians 5:20 says to always give thanks to God—for all things. *Give thanks for all things?* Give thanks for mosquitoes, parking tickets, cancer? Somehow choosing to be thankful in all things draws us closer to God—in ways that are sometimes surprising. For example, your son might not make the football team, but he could become an all-star on the soccer team.

Saying thank you to God for being God in every situation helps keep our hearts soft, our minds at peace, and our focus on what God freely gives us each day. We must remind our children that "all things work for good" and that God is always with us, even in our pain. Help your child be thankful for even the tough times because it is by them that we are driven into God's arms.

BIG BIBLE POINT

Remind your children "this is the day the Lord has made" (Psalm 118:24). Get them thinking about simple things to be thankful for!

- *What did God make?*
- *Are you alive?*
- *Do you have clean water and good food?*
- *Did you laugh today?*
- *How many friends and family members love you?*
- *What can we thank God for today?*

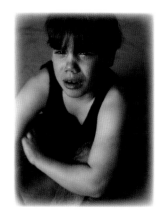

Be filled with hope.

Hope is not an innate thing; it is a choice. Can hope be learned? We get a clue from Romans 5:3, 4, which tells us to be glad for our problems because we know that they bring patience and patience brings experience and experience brings hope. Hope comes from going through tough times and seeing how God shows up. It may not happen the way you imagine, but God *will* be with you. Rich Mullins sang, "There's bound to come some trouble in your life"—and that's true. If you're breathing, you either have had problems, are in the middle of something tough, or soon will be.

key point
HOPE COMES FROM GOD.

The best way to teach your kids to have hope is to look for God's hand in any trial, not only in their lives but in yours as well. Remind them that God is always with them, no matter what happens. Teach your kids that the more they choose God, the more they will see Him. And that blessed assurance brings bushels of hope!

key point
TRUST GOD WITH YOUR TROUBLES.

It has been said that a person can live forty days without food, four days without water, four minutes without air, but not at all without hope!

Remind your kids that God is always with them, no matter what happens. Help them look for His hand at work. Doing so will build hope (and faith, too, by the way). Often God's hand is more easily seen in hindsight ... or at least that's when most of us see it, so don't stop looking!

TARGET MOMENT

Think about a difficult time ...

• How did you see God at work?
• Were there times when you felt God really close to you?
• What positives came from that time?
• What did you learn about hope?

Finally, you must teach your children to *choose* hope. Sure, some people seem more hopeful than others, but for the most part hopeful people are that way because they choose to be. They have seen God at work in their lives, and they believe what the Bible says: "In all things God works for the good of those who love him" (Romans 8:28), and they believe "that he who began a good work in you will carry it on to completion" (Philippians 1:6). They choose to look for God's hand at work in their lives right now. Practice looking for God's hand with your children ... every day ... in all things.

Remember: Teaching hope to your kids must begin with yourself. If you say you are hopeful, how do you show it?

Be hard working.

It's a common complaint: Kids today are lazy. They sit around and watch TV, play video games, or surf the Net. Are we doomed to have lazy kids who become lazy adults? Not necessarily. Encourage your child to help alongside you. Even toddlers can swish dusters and preschoolers mop the floor. They may splash more

than they scrub, but they'll be proud—and discover the fun of working.

key point
HARD WORK DEVELOPS A WORK ETHIC.

One expert suggests linking children's allowance or privileges to chores. In my early days, Thursday evenings were "Cleaning Nights." Mom turned on some lively music and set the timer. If we got all our jobs done before the timer went off, there was an extra scoop of ice cream as a reward.

TIPS FOR 'TWEENS
Give older kids the run of the kitchen for a meal. Let them plan a family meal or snack. Be prepared for boxed mac-'n-cheese, sandwiches, or popsicles! Praise the effort extravagantly. Of course, the grown-ups clean the kitchen afterwards!

Lemonade 10¢

Make working together fun *and* rewarding!

Don't underestimate your kids, but realize they probably won't do tasks as quickly or as well as you. Having jobs for your kids will build self-esteem and develop their ability to get things done. It's not always easy, but it is well worth it. Hard-working kids transition into hard-working adults. And the end result can be a sweet offering to God—and to busy parents!

key point
HELPING SERVES OTHERS —AND GOD!

Make work fun. Washing the car at our house often begins (or ends) in a water fight. Pulling weeds includes sitting in the sprinkler and eating watermelon afterward. You don't always have to bribe your children with money or treats, but always be grateful and praise them for their help. Often this is all it takes for them to willingly do more.

TRY THIS!

"Whatever you do, work at it with all your heart.... It is the Lord Christ you are serving."
(Colossians 3:23, 24)

Write household jobs on slips of paper. (Use different colors of paper for age-appropriate jobs.) Place them in a decorated jar. Let family members pull out jobs to do for extra cash, desserts, or a family trip to the movies.

VALUES ARE LEARNED, THEN LIVED.

Be humble.

The Bible warns against pride and teaches that first comes pride and then comes destruction (see Proverbs 16:18). What is the cure for pride? A little humility! Humility is seeing ourselves in a truthful light before the Creator of all things. But how can we teach humility to our kids with so much pride surrounding us?

> The interesting thing about humility is that once you think you have it, you probably don't!

The first step in teaching humility is to remind your children that life is not just about them. Our family uses the phrases "It's not about me" or "It's not about you" a lot. This isn't a put-down; it's a loving reminder that life is really *all about God*. Your children must learn that they are part of God's plan—not the other way around.

Ask your kids:

- Who is the most humble person you know? Why?
- How does giving God the credit draw us closer to Him?
- Is anyone bigger, smarter, or able to do more than God? Explain.
- How can we become more humble before God?

key point

HUMILITY IS PUTTING OTHERS FIRST.

"Every man is my superior in that I may learn from him."
—Thomas Carlyle

Certainly we don't want to stop praising our kids for fear we might give them a "big head," but remind them who gave them their abilities: "Sarah, you are an artist. God has given you such a gift!" Of course, the best way to teach humility is to model it. Discuss what a humble person looks like. Does he brag, "fish" for compliments, or try to be the center of attention? Of course not. But truly humble people aren't doormats either! They are strong and grateful to God for their salvation and know that God is in any good that is done.

key point
HUMILITY IS GIVING GOD THE CREDIT.

A Short Course in Human Relations

The 6 most important words:	**I ADMIT THAT I WAS WRONG.**
The 5 most important words:	**YOU DID A GREAT JOB!**
The 4 most important words:	**WHAT DO YOU THINK?**
The 3 most important words:	**COULD YOU PLEASE?**
The 2 most important words:	**THANK YOU!**
The most important word:	**WE**
The least important word:	**I**

Be joyful.

What's the difference between joy and happiness? Happiness comes from the outside, where external forces affect it. Joy comes from the heart—from knowing we belong to Christ! We can't manufacture joy, but it's not destroyed by outside factors. Dr. Adrian Rogers, a minister in Tennessee, concludes, "Happiness is like a thermometer: It just registers conditions. Joy is a thermostat that *controls* the conditions."

key point
JOY IS MORE THAN A FEELING.

Many parents have made *happiness* a priority in their kids' lives. They buy clothes, toys, and bikes as outward signs of happiness. But these items provide only fleeting happiness. It's a hard lesson to teach and accept, but God is not worried about our kids' happiness. He wants to fill them with something deeper. God wants us all to have *joy* in our lives!

HAPPINESS IS SURFACE AND CAN BE FLEETING ...

TRY THIS!

Make a special joy-filled spot in your home! Get a bulletin board and festive thumbtacks. Encourage the family to pin up joyful, encouraging notes, articles, cartoons, cards, pictures, or whatever you can think of that reminds your family of God's joy.

... TRUE JOY COMES FROM JESUS!

JOY SQUELCHERS

- *Watching "junk" on television.*
- *Consuming depressing news.*
- *Comparing your kids with others.*
- *Looking at what you don't have.*

We can help joy grow in our children. Ask the Holy Spirit to plant it in them, then get out of His way. Help them become aware of things that can take away joy: jealousy, an argumentative spirit, lying, unhealthy thoughts. Pray with your kids that God will help them clean their hearts, where the fruit of the Spirit can grow. Make a conscious effort to help your kids look at situations and people from a positive perspective. And teach your kids to give of themselves. Let them learn that serving others is serving Jesus. There really is no greater joy.

key point

JOY IS GREATER THAN HAPPINESS!

Happiness or joy—which do we desire? One makes us self-focused and vulnerable to bitterness. The other brings fulfillment, hope, and healing. Which do you choose for your life and the lives of your children?

JOY BOOSTERS

- *Helping someone less fortunate.*
- *Enjoying God's creation.*
- *Appreciating your kids as gifts.*
- *Looking at what God has given you.*

Be obedient.

Obedience can be difficult to teach. Perhaps this is because we, as parents, don't like to be the "bad guys," or because as humans, we don't like to obey. But the Bible says, "To obey is better than sacrifice" (1 Samuel 15:22). Let your kids know that God wants them to obey and that through obedience they demonstrate their love for you and for God.

key point
OBEDIENCE SHOWS LOVE AND RESPECT.

Help your kids learn that all choices—whether to obey or disobey—have consequences. Consider using "first-time obedience." Let your child know that if you must ask twice, there will be punishment. At each new stage in Meghan's development, we discuss what obedience is expected and what the punishment will be. This technique prevents the "I'm counting! 1-2-3 syndrome" and other equally exhausting parental experiments.

Steps for Dealing with a Stubborn 'Tween:

1. Figure out the areas where obedience is most lacking.

2. Visit with your child and explain what needs to be done to correct the problem and what the consequences will be if it isn't.

3. Write down both the problem area and the potential consequence.

4. Post it in a prominent place.

5. Be strong and consistent. Stick by your word.

6. Pray for yourself and your child to improve in this area and in obedience in general.

Kids need solid boundaries for disobedience, recognizing that consequences will vary with age and the offense. For example, we don't tolerate dishonesty, but a clean room isn't a big deal (unless company is coming). List what behaviors would result in the most severe punishments, such as dishonesty, being disrespectful, and treating another person (or his property) poorly.

Some punishments involve losing privileges, such as limiting video games to thirty minutes for a first offense and longer for the next one. Some parents dock allowances or give extra chores for disobedience. Consider having your children participate in setting their own punishments. This places the responsibility and choice to obey (or disobey) where it belongs—on their shoulders and in their hearts!

TARGET MOMENT

Check your own obedience level.

- **How do you show respect for authority at your job?**
- **How do you model respect for family members?**
- **How do you demonstrate obedience to God?**

key point
OBEDIENCE IS A CONSCIOUS CHOICE.

You can often gauge your own obedience by how you talk about those in authority over you.

Be patient.

We say and hear it enough: "Be patient!" But what *is* patience? In Greek, the word means "hanging on with feeling for a long time" or "cheerful, hopeful endurance." When we believe something good will come out of a situation, it is easier to "hang on." And each time we stretch our patience, it becomes stronger, longer, and more hopeful.

TIPS FOR TODDLERS

Try these tips for handling patience—with patience!

- **Be realistic in your expectations.** To a four-year-old, a "little while" may mean thirty seconds!

- **Keep your part of the bargain.** Kids need to know there actually will be a later time when you keep your word.

- **Involve your child in the process.** Kids are more patient when they have something to do.

- **Reward patience.** Do this instead of yelling when your child *isn't* patient.

We can help our kids learn patience by assuring they will receive what they are waiting for—within reason and time. God does answer prayer, but in His own time and way! Encourage patience if something is worth waiting for with great anticipation. For example, if your child is waiting for a new bike, say, "Just think of all the places you can go! Tell me what you'll do when you have your bike."

PATIENCE YIELDS

Strength
Faith
Perseverance
Persistence

Patience helps your child learn delayed gratification (something we adults aren't very good at). When your child wants to buy something special, help him make a chart to keep track as he saves up for it. Charting the dates and amounts saved will help your child see the progress of his patience—and it might help him see that patiently saving money is a good thing!

While waiting for your child, try saying: *"It's okay. I can wait. I'm patient."* This gives your child permission and respect—and also a model of what patience looks like.

key point
PATIENCE HELPS US LEAN ON GOD.

key point
PATIENCE TAKES TRUST AND HOPE.

Another kind of patience is the patience we have in suffering. Patience and grace can overcome rejection, self-doubt, and fears, thus providing growth and healing. This kind of patience can only be learned through experience. Developing patience in our kids takes time—and *patience!* Our job is to cheer them on when patience is on trial and applaud their successes along the way.

Elizabeth Carll, Ph.D., cautions, *"Teaching children patience is essential not only for school success but for development of appropriate interpersonal relationships and social skills. Poor impulse control can lead to aggression and violence for some children."*

Be persevering.

Remember the little engine that could? It chugged up the mountain and chanted, "I think I can! I think I can!" Although it took every ounce of her strength, she made it to the top. Winston Churchill once said, "Never give in. Never give in. Never, never, never, never—in nothing, great or small, large or petty—never give in." Perseverance is about never giving in—no matter what.

key point
JUST KEEP ON "KEEPIN' ON"!

If you or your child has ever been involved in a sport, you know how often you've been tempted to give up. Training for any event is never easy and often not fun. It requires hard work and perseverance. But to perform well, training must occur. The harder and longer a person trains, the easier the actual competition seems to be.

Perseverance is the "spiritual patience" that helps us hang on!

TIPS FOR TODDLERS
Read *The Little Engine That Could* and have your child repeat, "I think I can!" with you. Make "Little Engine That Could" awards out of blue ribbon to hand out when your child perseveres through something tough.

Any activity that requires commitment to "keep on keeping on" requires perseverance, including saving money, planting a garden, delivering papers, or babysitting. Discuss why it's important to keep persevering and not give up. Paul taught

Perseverance means running the good race without giving up!

that trials, or testing, help us develop "stick-to-it-iveness," which helps us grow to be strong. "No pain, no gain" is often true!

Join a team or club.

Learn to play a musical instrument.

PERSEVERANCE PROJECTS TO TRY!

Take up a new hobby.

Read through the Bible in a year!

Cheer your child on with phrases such as "I believe in you" and "Keep it up—you're doing great." Without perseverance, we fail to endure, we won't gain the needed skills to live for Jesus, and we might give up before the "good race" is over. Through perseverance, your child will be stretched and strengthened—and will experience victory to reward her hard work!

"By perseverance the snail reached the ark."
—Charles Spurgeon

Be peaceful.

We have a dog named Liberty who wags frantically when we come home. "Find the peace within, Libby," we laughingly say. It sounds rather "New Age-ish," but I think God wants us to do just that—find the peace within. Peace is a fruit of the Spirit within us, a gift the Prince of Peace (Jesus) gives us that Scripture tells us will guard our hearts and minds.

key point
ENCOURAGE PEACE TO GROW.

Is your home a place of peace? Pick a room and make it the Peaceful Place. Get rid of anything distracting in the room, including the television. Lower the lights when the family needs to relax. Now look at your family's schedule. Is there any time there for peace and reflection? Plan a family getaway to celebrate God's beautiful world, and let it sing to you and your children!

SCHEDULE TIME TO RELAX WITH YOUR FAMILY

Memorize Philippians 4:6, 7 as a family and repeat it often:
"Do not be anxious about anything, but in everything, by prayer and petition, with thanksgiving, present your requests to God. And the peace of God, which transcends all understanding, will guard your hearts and your minds in Christ Jesus."
(Learn Colossians 3:15 or 2 Thessalonians 3:16, too.)

Peace often comes with stillness. Set the timer for five minutes and sit outside with your kids. Don't say anything. Notice the sounds around you. Pray or just let your mind be quiet. Teach your kids the value of solitude. Remind your kids that "Jesus often withdrew to lonely places and prayed" (Luke 5:16). If the Son of God needed peaceful time away, we need it all the more!

Did you know that certain smells are very relaxing? Lavender is one of the best. Let your kids choose a scented candle or peaceful-smelling spray. Encourage your kids to feel at peace with a warm bath, a walk in the park, or hearing you read God's Word. Remind your kids that a heart of thankfulness helps the seeds of the peace and contentedness grow, even in stressful times.

COMFORT YOUR CHILD BY REMINDING HER OF PSALM 46:10: "BE STILL, AND KNOW THAT I AM GOD."

SET UP A "PEACE ROUTINE"—A SET OF ACTIVITIES THAT WILL HELP YOUR KIDS RELAX.

- Spray some lavender perfume on a pillow or favorite stuffed animal.
- Find peaceful music to play.
- Rub their backs or teach them some stretching exercises.
- Show them how to take slow, deep breaths.
- Pray with them for God to increase their peace.
- Suggest that they think of peaceful scenes or comforting Bible verses.

VALUES ARE LEARNED, THEN LIVED.

Be wise.

There are several ways to become wise. You can ask God for wisdom, as Solomon did. You can ask others for wisdom. This wise counsel allows us to gain from someone else's experience and knowledge, enabling us to make better decisions than we would have made alone. Almost anything you might experience has already been encountered by other members of God's family.

key point
SEEK GOD'S WISDOM IN ALL THINGS.

Finally, you can ask others to pray for you to receive wisdom: "The prayer of a righteous man is powerful and effective" (James 5:16).

key point
WISDOM IS MORE VALUABLE THAN GOLD!

No one has all wisdom, so don't be afraid to say to your child, "I don't know. Let's go find out." Teach him how to look on the Internet or visit the library to discover facts and information. But when your child needs wisdom of the heart about what Jesus would do, encourage him to consult the Bible and other Christian adults you both trust.

FORMULA FOR **GREAT WISDOM!**

Knowledge **FEAR OF THE LORD** Experience

WISDOM!

"The fear of the LORD is the beginning of wisdom." (Psalm 11:10)

Help your children understand that, although God loves them, they can't demand things from Him. He doesn't "owe" them anything; in fact, they owe Him everything. Teach your child that God helps us make wise decisions, which is why the Holy Spirit lives in us. When your child needs wisdom, encourage her to pray and ask God what to do. If she feels drawn toward a decision, then look up applicable Bible passages as she considers her options. Checking decisions against God's Word is the best litmus test in our search for wisdom!

Wisdom must be visible but not flaunted. If you don't know the answer to your child's question, find someone who does. Your child will actually love you more for it.

Enjoy these wise verses from Proverbs with your child!

PROVERBS 1:7

PROVERBS 2:10

PROVERBS 3:19

PROVERBS 4:5

PROVERBS 3:13, 14

PROVERBS 4:7

PROVERBS 8:11

PROVERBS 10:23

PROVERBS 16:16

Consider starting your day by discussing a bit of wisdom from Proverbs, then look for ways to apply that wisdom during the day.

PROVERBS 24:3

Valuing Honesty

"Nobody's perfect" we often say, but do we really believe it? We expect our children to never embarrass us, get straight A's, or make the all-star team. How do these unrealistic expectations make them feel about themselves, and what do they say about us?

Living honestly with yourself.

Trying to make ourselves and our children *look* perfect can cause stress and bring on all sorts of illnesses, both physical and mental. We must be honest with and about ourselves—only Jesus was and is perfect!

Take an honest look in the mirror.

Take a good, long look in the mirror. Who are you? Be honest. Get a piece of paper and list your personality assets and deficits. You might find that they are closely related. For instance, I'm a very "can do" person (which is a positive), but I can get pretty bossy when trying to get things done (negative!). The good news is: God loves our strengths, is undeterred by our weaknesses, and covers us completely with His grace.

key point

HONESTY OPENS THE HEART TO SERVE.

Discuss this quote from William Shakespeare with your kids: "This above all; to thine own self be true." What does it mean, and why is it important advice to follow?

TIPS FOR 'TWEENS

Have your 'tween draw a life-sized outline of himself on white shelf paper, then list on the drawing what he likes and dislikes about himself. Discuss the lists and how to change the negative qualities. Decorate the poster and hang it in your child's room.

key point
LIVING HONESTLY IS A POWERFUL WITNESS.

WE ALL HAVE ASSETS AND DEFICITS ... IF WE'RE HONEST. YET GOD LOVES US AS WE ARE!

How do you respond to your children's "assets" and "deficits?" Do you harp on weaknesses but ignore strengths, or praise strengths and ignore the weaknesses? When we honestly accept our kids for who they are, we become equipped to help them mature into healthy adults.

Guiding our kids to look at themselves in honest ways brings great benefits.

- *It makes them more dependent on God's grace.*
- *It makes them more grace-filled toward others.*
- *It invites the Holy Spirit to work in and through them.*

When we recognize our shortcomings and trust God to help, we find it easier to love, forgive, and grow. Such honest living allows your children to accept who they are, to humbly recognize God as perfect and powerful, and to serve others with genuine compassion.

SLIGHTLY OVER ONE-THIRD OF ADULTS (36%) ARE "SEARCHING FOR MEANING AND PURPOSE IN LIFE." WHAT DOES THIS SAY ABOUT HOW WE VIEW OUR LIVES?
(THE BARNA GROUP, 2001)

Handle emotions in positive ways.

Like you, your kids have times when they are in bad moods. They may have been hurt, feel down, or simply have gotten up on the wrong side of the bed and be grumpy. We often work hard at pretending that we are doing fine when we're really not. As parents, we can create a loving environment in which our children can share their pain and disappointments.

Have you ever *demanded* that your kids be okay? "Stop crying, it's not that awful!" "What's wrong with you? Straighten up!" Experience tells us that emotions aren't always easy to control. The key is to help our kids deal with their emotions by providing the right tools. If emotions are suppressed, depression often results. If they are denied, we may become psychotic. Emotions must be honestly dealt with.

key point
EMOTIONS ARE FROM GOD.

key point
CHANNEL ENERGY IN PLEASING WAYS.

TRY THIS!

When you're feeling down ...

- *Get away:*
  Take a walk.
  Go to your room.
- *Get it out:*
  Draw.
  Write in a journal.
  Do something active to blow off steam.
- *Get to God:*
  Tell God what you feel.
  Ask God what to do.

The challenge is to find the approach that best suits your child. Does she get angry often? Maybe running will give her the release she needs. Perhaps going a few rounds with a punching bag in the garage might help. Does he tend to get depressed? Painting, drawing, sculpting, or writing might help him explore what he is feeling. Do your kids resist any helpful suggestion? Have them change their environment by going for a walk or getting involved in some other activity. Encourage them to write down or make an audiotape of their feelings.

TARGET MOMENT

Being able to say "I'm not okay" helps your child let you know that something's wrong. Often just admitting that "I'm not okay" helps to release many of the negative feelings!

We feel what we feel—emotions may not always make sense, but they are valid. Often, just letting off steam can help the problem. Or pray with your child and remind him that emotions are God's gift to us—even the tough ones. Guide your child to identify times when he feels "not okay," then move ahead in transforming that energy into something helpful, creative, and good.

EMOTIONS ARE NATURAL. IT'S WHAT WE DO WITH THEM THAT IS EITHER GOOD OR BAD.

Living honestly with others.

Being real is often easier with your pet dog than with people. Humans expect so much from you. They can be hard to please, bossy, and insensitive. But remember: We can be that way, too!

Be realistic with expectations.

Expectations, disappointments, misunderstandings—being around people can be risky. Sometimes you get your feelings hurt, and sometimes you hurt someone else's feelings. How do you teach your kids to handle unreasonable teachers, hard coaches, and mean-spirited friends? (And what about hard-to-please parents, too?)

key point

EXPECTATIONS OFTEN DISAPPOINT.

"Truly loving another means letting go of all expectations. It means full acceptance, even celebration of another's personhood."
—Karen Casey

One reason we get our feelings hurt is because we have unrealistic expectations. Our child thinks a birthday should look a certain way. We think a spouse should act this way or a son should talk that way. Our notions of how people *should* behave or how something *ought* to look are often ideals—belonging to imaginary, perfect worlds where things never go wrong. When the ideal, or expectation, is not met, we often respond in anger or frustration. This is not to say that expectations are bad. Expectations can be good, but we need to teach our children to align them better with the real world and a godly perspective.

Help your child develop realistic expectations by talking about an anticipated event. For example, "What would you like for your birthday?" is a common question. When your child says he wants a pony, help him understand that such a gift may not be possible and why. Lovingly help your child replace out-of-reach ideals with realities. This same technique refocuses expectations a child might have about friends, family, or God.

BIG BIBLE POINT

Read aloud Psalm 5:3 to your child, then discuss the following about expectations we have surrounding God.

- *What can we expect from God?*

- *How do unrealistic expectations affect faith and trust?*

- *What are things God has promised us?*

- *Can we expect or trust God's promises to be kept? Explain.*

What can your kids do if people place unrealistic expectations on them? First, help them know that they are okay, since God loves them just as they are—and you do, too. Suggest that they consider whether the criticism or disappointment of others might be valid. Your goal is to help your children see themselves and others honestly. By taking the time to do this, you will help strengthen their self-esteem, make all their relationships stronger, and possibly prevent much pain.

- **Do you place unrealistic expectations on your family?**

- **Are you often disappointed in how things turn out?**

- **Do you feel that your children rarely try hard?**

- **Are you more critical of your mate than encouraging?**

Respect the people you disagree with.

If you hang around people for very long, someone somewhere will get angry and an argument will begin. At the very least, your kids will argue with you or with each other or with their friends. Can't we all just get along? Although conflicts will continue to arise, we can learn to disagree without devastating each other.

key point
CONFLICTS HAPPEN.

Give your kids verbal "traffic signals" to help them deal with impending conflict:

Red Light—Stop. Take deep breaths. Calm down.

Yellow Light— Slow down. Think. Discuss.

Green Light—Go ahead and try the best plan.

There are rules to a good fight—or rather, a good disagreement! First, choose to respect each other. Reminding the other person that you value his opinions diffuses many disagreements, and the "battle" becomes an opportunity to understand one another. Next, don't assign blame but try to be specific: only one disagreement at a time. Finally, listen to the other person with openness and respect.

key point

CONFLICTS HELP US GROW.

Try to brainstorm ideas on how to solve the problem of your disagreement peaceably. When you're wrong, seek forgiveness and apologize. Help your child realize that there is nothing more healing than to say (or hear), "I was wrong. Will you forgive me?" This is especially true when dealing with your children, and it provides a powerful role model for them to emulate!

Kids often find themselves in situations that start out as horseplay and escalate into real arguments. In cases such as this, our family uses the phrase "for real." This informs the other person that emotions are becoming negative—in a real and honest way. Use the conflict to share openly with one another and end in a prayer asking for God's grace.

WHAT KIND OF FIGHTER ARE YOU (AND YOUR KIDS)?

- **Insane Machine Gunner:** blasting everything in your path

- **Methodical Sniper:** looking for the opponent's weak link

- **AWOL:** running away or avoiding conflict at all costs

- **Water-Gun Clown:** avoiding conflict with sarcastic humor

- **Mount Vesuvius:** letting things build up until you blow your top

By the way, none of these is very helpful in dealing with conflict. Ask God for patience and understanding instead!

Living honestly with God.

God knows everything about you. He knows your good parts and your yucky parts. And here's the kicker—there is nothing you can do that will make God love you any more or any less than He does right now!

Know the value of God's acceptance.

Do you remember the story *The Velveteen Rabbit*? It's about a stuffed bunny that wants to become real. The bunny is dragged about by a little boy until it is ultimately loved to tatters. Finally, the old bunny is thrown on the trash. But that night, a fairy gives the bunny his deepest wish: he becomes real through the love of the boy.

Your child needs to know he is made "real" by God's love and acceptance! God made us (Psalm 139:13) and called us by name (John 10:3). God made us inside and out and knows our every thought—good and bad. Read Psalm 139:1-10 with your child, then assure him that God knows everything there is to know about him … and loves him anyway.

key point
GOD LOVES YOU PERFECTLY— RIGHT NOW!

> "Deep down even the most hardened criminal is starving for the same thing that motivates the innocent baby: love and acceptance."
>
> —Lily Fairchilde

Understanding the truth about God's love and acceptance helps to make us *real*. When our children truly see themselves and know that God loves and accepts them no matter what, they learn to love themselves—even if who we are isn't always lovely. We want our kids to learn that being real is healthy and that it's okay to accept God's love.

How do you teach being real to your kids? You will have to be real yourself. No excuses for bad behavior. When you are wrong, say you're sorry. Stop doing things just because they make you look good. No yelling at your kids because you're having a bad day. Talk it out with them. Ask for their help. They will learn to be real when they see the beauty of you being real with yourself, your family, and God.

key point
GOD ACCEPTS YOU.

Remind your kids that being real doesn't mean they can't change hairstyles or try new fashions—it's about what motivates the change. It shouldn't be to gain the acceptance of others or to follow the crowd but rather to become the best person one can be—from the inside out!

Unconditional love means accepting the good with the bad. That's the love God has for us!

Value grace even though it's not deserved!

Grace is undeserved love, mercy, and forgiveness from God to us. Grace isn't deserved and can't be earned. One preacher gave this example: "If our youth minister stole money from the church, justice would be to fire him, mercy would be to let him continue to work here … but grace would be to let him still work *and* give him a raise!"

Grace demonstrates forgiveness, empathy, and compassion!

key point
GRACE IS UNDESERVED FAVOR.

key point
GOD OFFERS GRACE FREELY.

Living in a stubborn state of not offering forgiveness or grace can lead to self-righteousness, pride, and hypocrisy. We want our kids to avoid having the attitude that everyone "gets what they deserve!" When someone speeds by, do you wish for a police officer magically to appear? What about when you are zipping along? Don't you hope the police are in the next county? Grace changes how we view ourselves and one another.

"For it is by grace you have been saved, through faith" (Ephesians 2:8). Read the verses below about grace with your child and discuss what we can learn about God and His love.

- ❤ Ephesians 1:7, 8
- ❤ Ephesians 2:8-10
- ❤ Romans 6:14
- ❤ Romans 9:8
- ❤ Romans 12:6

Can we teach our children to be grace-filled when we aren't? No, but we can learn to be grace-filled together. Growing the value of grace means offering forgiveness even when it's hard or not deserved. If your child does something that merits punishment, offer forgiveness and grace instead. Point out that punishment is deserved but that you are offering the gift of grace this time. As kids begin to see grace in everyday situations, they will begin to understand more about God's gift of forgiveness for their sins.

TIPS FOR 'TWEENS

'Tweens need lots of grace! Their bodies are beginning to change, schoolwork is more demanding, and their emotions swing when they're expected to control them. Share time and talk with your 'tween. Remember that grace is a huge part of loving relationships!

"Grace substitutes a full, childlike and delighted acceptance of our need, a joy in total dependence. We become 'jolly beggars.' "

—C. S. Lewis

GETTING GRACE

- Pray for your family to be drawn closer to God.
- Ask God to help you all understand grace more.
- Find times to talk with your kids about grace and what it means.
- Freely offer grace as an example of Christ's love.
- Ask your kids to offer grace to others.
- Help kids see others in a grace-filled light.

Do your children remind you of the wrongs committed against them? Do they get angry when asked to think beyond their own wants and needs? Look for moments to give your kids grace, but urge them to offer understanding, forgiveness, and grace to others—especially their siblings. True grace offers empathy toward others even when it may not be deserved.

Dishonesty cheats everyone.

Dishonesty runs rampant in our culture. We fib and tell "little white lies." We bring "a few things" home from the office instead of buying the supplies. We "help" our kids with their school projects (translation: we do the work so they will "look good" and it takes less time). We let our kids "cut and paste" stuff from the Internet so reports can be finished quickly.

key point
DISHONESTY KILLS TRUST.

TARGET MOMENT

35 percent of Christians versus 57 percent of non-Christians feel that, to get by these days, you may have to bend the rules for your own benefit. What does this tell us about integrity as a "valued" value?
(The Barna Group, 1997)

TRY THIS!

Make dishonesty a big deal in your house—even with toddlers. If your child tells a lie, encourage him to confess to the one lied to and seek forgiveness. Support him through this time of repentance, pray with him, and go along to make amends. Remind your child that lying (or cheating or stealing) moves us away from God.

There is a steep price for even small acts of dishonesty. When you know someone has lied to you, it's hard to trust that person again. Sometimes the relationship completely dies. And dishonesty separates us from God. We try to hide it and deny ourselves a deeper relationship with Him. Even though dishonesty can start small, it often builds quickly as we look the other way.

key point

INTEGRITY SHOWS RESPECT.

THE TRUTH IS ...

16% of Americans say that "whatever works in their life" is the only truth that they know.

7% of Americans report that lying is sometimes necessary.

6% of Americans say that if a cashier gave them too much change, they'd just let it go.

Ephesians 4:25 (*The Message*)
"What this adds up to, then, is this: no more lies, no more pretense. Tell your neighbor the truth. In Christ's body we're all connected to each other, after all. When you lie to others, you end up lying to yourself." **How are you doing? "Pretense" means living another life. Are you saying one thing but living another? Are you the same at work and at church? Do you tell the truth in love? We must be diligent in honesty.**

We have a responsibility to teach our children the value of integrity—of not cheating, stealing, or lying. If a child cheats in school, he must face his teacher, and a parent should accompany him. If a child steals, accompany him to admit his offense. Is this really such a big deal? Yes, it is a big deal, and yes, people "fib" or "cheat a little" all the time. But no excuse warrants lying, cheating, or stealing!

Ask God to show you your own "white lies" and where you may be setting a bad example, then correct those areas. Give your children real-life examples of the value of integrity. Tell stories of people who were honest. And encourage integrity when it is needed most—if a wallet is found, a friend has been lied about, or a cause of Christ is at stake.

Valuing Love

It has been said that if Christ hadn't been nailed to the cross, His love for us would have held Him there. Love is the most powerful force on earth. With it, shattered lives are healed, huge barriers are torn down, hard hearts are softened, and eternities are altered.

Learning to accept love.

It's worth saying again: There is nothing you can do that will make God love you more or less than He does right now. We must plant this truth deep into our children's hearts, since it is the one truth that disarms evil and allows Christlike values to grow in your child's life!

Accept God's love.

key point

WE CAN'T EARN GOD'S LOVE.

Before kids can grow Christlike values in their lives, they must be able to openly accept God's love and see themselves as God's gifts. Satan would love nothing more than to stop your child from becoming what God desires him to be—and love is a virtue to stop those lies!

WE MAY NOT BE WORTHY, BUT WE ARE FAR FROM WORTHLESS!

key point

ACCEPTANCE ALLOWS US TO GROW!

How can we help our children accept God's love and reject the lies? Tell them the truth. They can't work hard enough to earn God's love or salvation. God placed great value on us when He paid for our sins with His Son's life.

Look in your child's eyes and tell her *specifically* what you love about her. Point out that God made her fearfully and wonderfully (read Psalm 139 as a powerful reminder). Listen when your child talks about herself and correct her if she says, "I'm worthless." After all, God doesn't make junk!

key point

WE CAN ACCEPT GOD'S LOVE.

LOVE JARS
Let each person decorate a jar and lid. On slips of paper, write five qualities you see in yourself and in each person, such as, "You're a hard worker." Place the papers in the jars to pull out and read each day. Add new ones every week.

- Do you accept yourself as worthwhile?
- Can you accept God's love into your life?
- How does loving yourself allow you to love others?
- What are your best qualities?
- How can you use them to serve God and others?

Don't confuse self-abasement with humility. Truly humble people understand their need for a relationship with God, and they are glad for God's love, acceptance, and grace. Helping your child accept God's love opens the door for growing values such as faith, trust, forgiveness, compassion, and a spirit of serving—which is what love is all about!

Learn to love what God gave you.

God has given us so much, if we will just stop to see it. Sometimes we're so busy surviving that we forget to appreciate all God has done for us!

Appreciate God's gifts.

God's creativity shows up everywhere. Just look at the people in your family. Each person looks different, sounds different, and acts differently. Psalm 139:13, 14 tells us, "For you created my inmost being.... Your works are wonderful." It's important for your child to see and appreciate how God made us unique and to enjoy the differences.

We must learn to appreciate the good in each other, for God gave each of us as gifts to the world!

To grow the value of appreciation, your child needs to take a closer look at how God has made each person unique. Friends and family are gifts that God created as different as snowflakes. Remind your child that his friends are personal gifts from God, as is the family he was born into. Encourage your child to take time to be grateful for what God has given!

key point
YOU ARE A GIFT FROM GOD!

TARGET MOMENT

Help your child realize there are so many gifts to appreciate, including ...

- family
- Jesus
- ice cream and pizza
- summer vacation
- your family pet
- friends
- salvation

God has offered each of us salvation, has adopted us as His children, and has given the Holy Spirit to live within us. We need to highlight those gifts for our kids often, reminding them that John was right when he wrote: "How great is the love the Father has lavished on us, that we should be called children of God! And that is what we are!" (1 John 3:1).

To help your family appreciate God's gifts, make pictures or posters that focus on the blessings God has given you. If you have a child who likes to work on the computer, have him design an appreciation page focused on God's gifts. Then print out the page for friends and family. Everyone needs to be reminded often to appreciate all God has done for us!

BE THANKFUL FOR HIS GIFTS.

WHAT PART ARE YOU?

On shelf or butcher paper, draw a life-sized outline of a person. Let kids decorate it if they want to. Take turns assigning members of your family and friends to the various body parts. For example, your daughter might love soccer, so she could be one of the feet. Or your son might always pitch in with the chores, so he could be a hand. Christ should be the head of a family, but there are many parts left!

Care for creation!

God made everything and saw that it was good. He told Adam to take care of it and to name the parts of creation. Nature sings of God's handiwork and waits for Christ's return. There's much to learn and enjoy if we consider creation not only as a gift but as a description of our Creator.

key point
VALUE NATURE.

key point
NATURE IS GOD'S CREATIVITY!

Nothing comes more naturally than kids wanting to praise God for His wondrous world—and you can help develop the qualities of good-earth stewardship. If your child is fascinated with animals, watch nature shows together. Ask your child to teach you about his favorite animals—you might be amazed at what he knows! Does he wonder why God created a certain fish? Brainstorm or research possible answers.

TARGET MOMENT

Provide a place to show off some of God's creation. Have a shelf or interesting tray that displays your family's collection of unusual rocks, leaves, or pictures of sunsets and clouds.

"I love to think of nature as an unlimited broadcasting station, through which God speaks to us every hour, if we will only tune in."
—George Washington Carver

Everything God made has a purpose. From flowers to fleas, from molehills to mountains, God has a plan for creation, and we can care for the wonders in it. Encourage your child to explore nature in books, on the Internet, or in real life! Imagine with your child how God might have enjoyed making the earth and all that was in it. (How did He think up the kangaroo or platypus, anyway?)

Teach your children to enjoy nature. Spend time walking, hiking, climbing, and fishing. See who can spot the most animals, the tallest tree, or the prettiest leaf. Point out that nature gives proof of the Creator (Romans 1:20) and waits for God's future glory (Romans 8:22). Encourage your child to recycle, reuse, and respect God's creation. By caring for nature, our kids will see God all around them!

BIG BIBLE POINT

Read Genesis 1:26 with your child, then discuss why God gave humans responsibility over the earth and the things in it. Name ways you can help care for the earth, such as:

- picking up trash
- keeping air clean
- planting trees and flowers
- keeping water clean

TRY THIS!

Take white paper and crayons on a walk. Instead of picking up a log, place paper over its bark and rub the side of a crayon over the paper. Use different colors for various rubbings on the same paper. Frame your rubbings for everyone to enjoy.

Express yourself to honor God.

When God said, "Let us make man in our image…" (Genesis 1:26), we were given special characteristics that no other part of creation has. One of those characteristics is the desire to create. Francis Schaffer asserts that "We never find an animal, non-man, making a work of art. On the other hand, we never find men anywhere in the world or in any culture in the world who do not produce art." Creativity is a gift from God that sets us apart in creation.

key point
CREATE FOR GOD'S JOY!

How can we encourage our children to develop creative expression and focus it toward God? First of all, make sure they have supplies so they can find their own medium. Modeling clay, wood scraps, paper, paints, and boxes excite budding sculptors. A pretend microphone might be inspiration to a young troubadour. Ask your child about his creative work and to share his feelings as he develops ways to express himself.

"The Christian is the one whose imagination should fly beyond the stars."
—Francis Schaeffer

- Visit an art museum. God gave artists expressive gifts. How many types of art do you notice?
- Play a recording of Handel's *Messiah*. Handel wrote much of his music as an expression of love for God.

key point
EXPRESS YOUR HONOR TO GOD.

And here's the most beautiful thing: although creating something and showing it to someone is wonderful, as God's children we're to create things for God's pleasure. In other words, whether anyone ever sees our drawings or sculptures, our expressions are complete if we created them to honor God! Encourage your child to paint God a picture, write Him a poem, or pen a song to our Father.

Using creativity to honor and worship God nurtures the values of gratitude, thanksgiving, and celebration—all rolled into one! Encourage family members to interpret a favorite Scripture in a new way or make a picture that illustrates one of God's many names. "And whatever you do, whether in word or deed, do it all in the name of the Lord Jesus, giving thanks to God the Father through him" (Colossians 3:17).

TIPS FOR TODDLERS

- Lucy Micklethwait has written a series of *I Spy* books for art. They're a fun way to get kids to look at great art.
- Play the Silly Dance game! Have someone "man" the radio. When the music starts, everyone dances in the way the music makes him feel. Change the station for more "interpretive" fun!

EXPRESS YOURSELF!

Create collages using cast-away items.

Make a home movie.

Make a bread-dough sculpture.

Write a poem or song.

Value and share God's gifts.

God blesses us with many good things, but we aren't to keep those blessings to ourselves. Through values such as serving, compassion, and generosity God helps us bless others.

Reach out with compassion.

We might not understand it, but God has a purpose for everything (Ecclesiastes 3:1). It's the same with the blessings God gives His people. God said to Abraham, "I will make you into a great nation and I will bless you" (Genesis 12:2). Jesus urged his followers to bless others by serving them and showing great compassion. If we're to teach our children to have the values God desires, we want to encourage our kids to serve others, too.

Share your gardening talents—plant or weed an elderly neighbor's flower garden!

Each time your child shows compassion for someone, let him put a sticker on a calendar. When a month of stickers are collected, let your child choose a special treat.

Share this phrase with your children: "You are blessed to be a blessing." God provides wonderful blessings for His children, and in turn our children can be blessings to others. Ask your kids to look at your neighborhood. Are there elderly people who could use a helping hand? Is someone sick and could use a meal? Help your child become a "Blessing Patrol" looking for ways to bless others.

Of course, teaching your kids to be a blessing can be costly—not just in money, but in time and effort. It means that parents need to be encouraging and be ready to help our kids help others. We might need to help make cookies or babysit. But the values our kids nurture when they offer compassion and the blessings they become to others are well worth it!

key point
REACH OUT WITH CONCERN.

80% of evangelical Christians have shared their faith with a non-Christian in the past year.
(The Barna Group)

Kids sharing their compassion go a long way in bringing the Good News about Jesus!

Share with your child the parable of the Good Samaritan (Luke 10:25-37). Discuss how the people who should have cared didn't, but the one whom no one thought would care, did. We must be on the lookout for ways to show compassion to all people.

Caring for others is paramount in God's plan, and starting close to home is great. Let your children invite friends and families to special events at church. Tell them about Jesus and ask if you can help in any way. Every little effort creates an opportunity for kids to reach out to others. Caring, concern, and compassion are great ways to "put skin on" the words "God is love."

Sharing with brothers and sisters shows compassion, too!

Reach out with generosity.

key point

KIDS CAN MAKE A DIFFERENCE.

God wants us to bless not only our neighbors but people across the globe. That seems like a very big job, but teaching our children that God can do amazing things with one willing heart makes a big job seem possible. Here's how one boy with a willing heart changed a needy village forever.

A six-year-old boy named Ryan heard about children dying in Africa due to unclean water. He did extra chores and raised $70. When he found out that a large well would cost $25,000, he decided to do more chores. More and more people found out and offered to help. Six years later, Ryan has been seen by over 100 million people through TV interviews and newspaper

and magazine stories. Nearly $1 million has been raised by a little boy who prayed, "Please, God, let every kid in Africa have clean water." (Could our kids, too, do amazing things if we encouraged them?) Ryan's parents supported their son's desire to raise money and awareness for the wells. They helped by sending out e-mails and making phone calls. Although they were afraid Ryan might fail, they felt he had to try.

key point

BE GENEROUS WITH LOVE!

EVEN ONE PERSON CAN CHANGE SOMEONE'S WORLD!

How can we reach out with generosity? First of all, begin to pray together for people around the world. There are several books that describe different cultures of the world in language your child will understand. Consider purchasing one of these books or use an atlas as a prayer guide for your family. Remind your child that God hears our prayers of intercession and helps you spread His love around the world.

Adopt a Compassion kid (www.compassion.com) and have your child write letters to her long-distance "sibling." Discuss world events and pray about ways to help. Two kids in Houston, Texas (ages 9 and 6), decided to help the tsunami victims. Selling lemonade, they raised over $3,000 to generously give to the American Red Cross!

key point
PRAY FOR EVERYONE IN THE WORLD.

TARGET MOMENT

• **Be generous with your love:** "Adopt" a needy child.
• **Be generous with your time:** Serve at a soup kitchen.
• **Be generous with your resources:** Donate to a service organization.
• **Be generous with your faith:** Pray for others in the world.

Is there something you could sacrifice to help someone in need? Even $10 a week can change a life on the other side of the world!

Remind your child that we do everything in Jesus' name. It's one thing to do good things for people, but if it doesn't bring them closer to Jesus, it will only help them for a little while. They will still spend eternity lost. By using generosity and love, your child can make a difference in the lives of people he may not even know—but whom Jesus does!

Reach out as Jesus reached out.

key point
GIVE OF YOUR TIME AND TALENTS.

key point
SHARE JESUS WITH OTHERS.

Generously giving time and money may be difficult, but there are different ways to reach out to others. Paul tells us in Philippians that Epaphroditus almost died for the work of Christ. Epaphroditus brought money, but he also brought much more. He brought *himself*. We must remember that whatever we do should be done in the name of Jesus. And as Jesus reached out lovingly to others with help, healing, and Himself—so can we!

How do we teach our kids to do everything in Jesus' name? First, sit down with your children and plan how to keep the focus on Jesus when doing a good deed. You may want to say to the receiver outright, "This is from Jesus." You may prefer to write a note that says, "We are doing this because we love you and because Jesus loved us." Some people give silver crosses that say "Jesus Loves You" along with a gift. Others give small Bibles or selected scriptures. You may not feel the time is right to say anything at all. But whatever it is, be sure you do all things in Jesus' name—and power.

Jesus helped others as a carpenter, but how else did he reach out?
• He healed them. (Matthew 9:22)
• He fed them. (Matthew 14:19)
• He gave life. (Romans 6:4)
• He prayed. (John 17:20, 21)
How can you reach out to others?

 Treat others as if they were Jesus!

> **"PREACH THE WORD IN EVERY WAY; IF NECESSARY, USE WORDS."**
>
> **—MOTHER TERESA**

Another way to teach your child to reach out in Jesus' name is to go with her on a short-term missions trip. Getting your children out of their zip code and comfort zone can do amazing things for them! It opens their hearts. It gives them a larger worldview. It might even plant a seed that will grow to produce a great servant for Christ!

Check with your church to find out what mission organizations they support. Often they will have special speakers or special collection drives in which your kids could participate. (Our church just had the grade-school kids collect money for shoes.) Experience how working with others makes a larger difference!

TRY THIS!

Pick an organization that allows for specific giving, such as shoes. Ask the organization for a video so your child can see what he or she is giving toward. Decorate a box and put extra change in it. For each dollar collected, add a sticker to the box until your giving goal is reached.

Reaching out, whether by giving or by going, makes for a better, more mature person, no matter the age. Look in the "More Resources" section for some short-term mission groups or contact your church and pray with your kids about reaching out to others and sharing Christ. It takes effort and sacrifice, but it will be worth it!

Show and tell your values!

We show our inner values and love in many ways. Forgiveness, friendships, accepting others, and listening are all "habits" of love your child can nurture in his life—then pass on to others!

Accept others as Jesus accepts you.

In today's mobile society, we're exposed to many cultures and diverse opinions. Jesus wants us to accept others, but where do we draw lines that accept others without changing our own values? How can we teach our kids to love and help their neighbors and others in healthy ways? The best way is to spend time with your kids and help develop their Christian walk.

BIG BIBLE POINT

Jesus said not to judge or we would be judged (Matthew 7:1). Ask your child how not judging plays a role in how we accept others. Can we judge others and still accept them? Ask your child what might have happened if Jesus had not accepted us. Would we live close to God? Remember: God loves us even with our shortcomings. We must do the same for others regardless of how different from us they may seem.

key point
JESUS ACCEPTED US.

God wants us to love people and draw them to Him … whatever they look like, however they act. Unfortunately, love and acceptance are often conditional. Teach your child that real love is often "in spite of" rather than "because of." Remind your child that God loved us while we were still doing wrong (Romans 5:8), and He wants us to love and accept others unconditionally, too.

Do you feel comfortable around people of different cultures, who dress differently, and are of different faiths? Attend ethnic festivals with your child. Discuss the ethnic background of each festival, ask questions of the people there, try the foods. Or take your kids to various ethnic restaurants. Learning about people around the world will help your kids understand people who are different than they are.

TRY THIS!

Find a dark place to sit with your child and a flashlight. Flip off the light and chat about how darkness is like someone not being accepted by others. Remind your child that Jesus said we are "the light of the world" (Matthew 5:14). Turn on the light. Remind your child that when we accept others it's like turning on the light of love in their world!

Accepting people and their differences is one of the most Christlike things we can do. When your child talks about someone at school who is different or an outcast, encourage him to get to know that person better. Your child can become a beacon of Jesus' light and love by accepting others as Jesus accepted us. This is the beginning of true compassion in action!

key point
EXPERIENCE OTHER CULTURES.

key point
WE CAN ACCEPT OTHERS.

How accepting are you? What goes through your mind when you see someone of another ethnic background or someone with many piercings? Are your thoughts those of curiosity or judgment? Acceptance is vital to us as Christians!

Forgive yourself.

Self-condemnation is a negative emotion that threatens to block the growth of Christlike values in our kids. When we condemn ourselves, we are refusing God's love and forgiveness. In essence, we're telling God: "You *say* you forgive me, but you don't *really* know what I've done and what I'm like." This attitude can unknowingly be passed on to our kids. Self-condemnation is one of Satan's craftiest tools.

TRY THIS!

Help your child stop self-defeating thoughts. Let him wear a rubber band on his wrist. If he has a thought he knows is a lie, tell him to snap the rubber band—snap, there goes the lie!

BIG BIBLE POINT

Share Psalm 103:12 with your child and remind him that God has forgiven him through Jesus and remembers his sins no more! If God and Jesus have forgiven him—he can forgive himself as well.

We need to stop self-deprecation in our kids before the walls against values are built—but how? First, we must identify the lies we believe. Have you ever told your kids they are hopeless, either with words or actions? Kids pick up on our words and feelings more than we sometime think. Be positive and genuinely compliment your kids. Turn the cycle of lies into truth!

key point
CONFESS AND FORGIVE YOURSELF.

key point
JESUS HAS FORGIVEN US.

As parents, we must be on the lookout as our children talk. When we hear negative talk or recognize depression or fear in our children, we can assure them that God has forgiven them, we have forgiven them, and they must forgive themselves. Explain that when we forgive ourselves, we can begin to forgive others as Jesus has forgiven us.

Forgiving ourselves and teaching our children to do the same is amazingly healing. Remember that forgiveness does not mean excusing poor behavior or explaining it away. But teaching our kids to admit to sin, give it to God, and forgive themselves will take away a tool Satan regularly uses against us all!

LIST THINGS YOU WANT TO FORGIVE YOURSELF FOR. PRAY AND GIVE THEM TO GOD BY TAPING THE PAPER TO A HELIUM BALLOON AND RELEASING IT. IMAGINE GOD CATCHING THEM AS YOU RELEASE THEM. EVEN TODDLERS CAN SEND "I'M SORRY" MESSAGES TO GOD THIS WAY!

PARENTS POINTER

Although it may seem there couldn't be much your child needs to forgive in himself, you might be surprised. Listen closely to what even your young ones say. Some kids are down on themselves from a very early age.

Our words have great power to bless or to curse. What do your words say to your child?

Forgive others.

Ann Landers once said, "One of the secrets of a long and fruitful life is to forgive everybody everything every night before you go to bed." Not being forgiven or needing to forgive someone shackles us to festering emotions and cages us with negative memories. It eats away at our hearts, minds, and relationships. How can we teach our children to stay free from this prison?

Failure to forgive locks away emotions—and love!

key point
FORGIVE AS JESUS FORGAVE YOU.

TARGET MOMENT

Help kids forgive someone in a concrete way by writing that person's name on paper. Share a prayer that God will help your child forgive completely. Then wad up the paper and toss it in the trash or burn it, saying, "I forgive you in the name of Jesus Christ."

It has been said that forgiveness is not an emotion; it's a decision. Maybe that's why it's hard to offer. Anger, resentment, and hurt can get the best of us. To teach our children forgiveness, we must practice it. Take time to pray about those whom you may need to forgive. Then make a decision to give up the hurt you received from that person. Choose to forgive.

"Forgive, and you will be forgiven." (Luke 6:37)

When your child is wronged, try to address her reaction as soon as possible. Talk about the offense and how it made her feel. Hold your child close. And ask her to pray for God's help in forgiving the person. Some personalities forgive more easily than others. Your child may need to pray several times. Or send the offense to God by writing it on a helium-filled balloon and releasing it. She could even write on a rock and toss it in a lake. It often helps young ones to visualize the act of forgiveness.

key point
FORGIVENESS
FREES
LOVE.

Researcher Richard Fitzgibbons cites these benefits to the one who forgives:

DECREASED LEVELS OF ANGER AND HOSTILITY

IMPROVED PHYSICAL HEALTH

ENHANCED CAPACITY TO TRUST

INCREASED FEELINGS OF LOVE

IMPROVED ABILITY TO CONTROL ANGER

FREEDOM FROM EVENTS OF THE PAST

Seeking and offering forgiveness between siblings is critical. Suggest that the offending party look the other in the eye and say, "I was wrong. I am sorry." Then ask the other child to look the offender in the eye and say, "I forgive you." Afterwards, encourage hugs. By eye contact and hugging, healing often happens quickly and resentment is avoided. Keeping your children's hearts soft toward each other will help them remain close to each other throughout their lives.

Value good friendships.

Being a friend takes work. You must find out what other people like and don't like. You must learn their opinions on all sorts of topics. And you may not agree with them. Kids love being friends with others and are beginning to understand the value of friendship. Even early friendships help kids recognize that to have a friend we must be a friend.

key point
GET TO KNOW EACH OTHER!

**Deep friendship is rare—
but worth the effort!**

TIPS FOR 'TWEENS
Help your 'tween become more understanding. When she tells you about a difficult incident in school or church, ask:
- *How do you think the other person felt?*
- *What do you think this person was thinking?*
- *What do you wish you could say to this person?*

Then pray with your child.

key point
BE A FRIEND, HAVE A FRIEND.

Teaching your child to be a good friend involves helping her understand her friends. One way to is to ask how her friend feels about various issues. It may begin with simple things such as her favorite color or flavor of ice cream. Even simple things shared will help your child care more deeply for her friends and give everyone more grace when miscommunications happen.

TIME + KNOWLEDGE + GRACE = UNDERSTANDING

How about friendship between siblings? Often we are kinder to strangers than we are to members of our family. Find ways for your family to learn about each other. Make a list of questions to discuss during dinners. Encourage each child to tell about a favorite moment of his or her day. Discourage teasing. When differences are respected and feelings are expressed in safety, even siblings become better friends!

Your toddler may want to show his love for a friend by coloring a special picture or sharing a cookie. Or let your toddler dictate a note to mail to his friend. Always praise your child for thinking of others!

key point
FRIENDS SHOW PATIENCE.

Your children might find themselves in a group where they are with a wide variety of people. This can cause misunderstandings and stress. Help your child focus on the similarities of the group rather than the differences of individuals. Pray with your child about the group. As the team learns to work together, differences can often disappear as friendships start to bloom.

TO BECOME CLOSE FRIENDS, DECIDE THAT YOU MAY NOT AGREE ON EVERY-THING BUT WILL LOVE EACH OTHER ANYWAY.

TABLE TALK FOR FRIENDLY FAMILIES:

- Grossest food eaten
- Scariest moment
- Favorite movie and why
- Place in the world you want to visit
- Favorite book or character

Value good listening.

key point
GOOD LISTENING SHOWS RESPECT.

Listening is different from hearing. When you hear something, sound waves enter your ear canal and register with your brain. Listening, on the other hand, demands that you interact with what is making the sounds. Communication experts say that listening is more important than speaking. If so, how do we teach our kids the value of good listening skills?

First, practice good listening habits yourself. A good listener looks at the speaker. When your child is talking to you, face her and look into her eyes. This will send a strong message that you are really engaged in what is happening. Kids need to realize that good listening shows respect. Listen to your kids, and they'll value listening to you!

TRY THIS!

At dinner, give one sentence describing a "mystery item" such as, "I'm thinking of an animal…." Then go around the table, allowing each person to ask a question. (No one can guess the animal or item until everyone asks one question.) Encourage everyone to listen carefully! Then allow the youngest to have the first guess or ask another question.

Experts say that listening is more important than speaking; maybe that's why God gave us two ears and only one mouth!

key point
GOOD LISTENING SHOWS LOVE.

Good listeners maintain an open body posture where their arms are not crossed. A defensive stance means we *might* be hearing someone— but we're probably not listening well. Watch your child with his peers; you might see that he is much more fierce in his communication with others. If so, remind him that being a good friend means being a good listener.

PRACTICE GOOD LISTENING!

LOOK at the person speaking.

Put your **HANDS** on your lap.

Nod and **SMILE** to signal you're listening.

Do **NOT INTERRUPT** the speaker.

Though it's often hard for kids to listen rather than talk, remind your child that a good listener values hearing what the other person has to say and doesn't interrupt. Encourage your child to rephrase what was just said. For example, if someone says, "I hate school," your child might respond by saying, "It sounds like you've had a hard day—want to talk about it?"

Remind your child that demonstrating the value of being a good listener shows respect. Encourage your child to take time to listen to each family member this week. Challenge him to discover something new about each person. Then have him do the same with friends at school. Taking time to listen not only shows respect; it shows kindness, genuine interest, and will help your child become an active listener as he grows up.

Love your enemies.

"**Y**ou have heard that it was said, 'Love your neighbor and hate your enemy.' But I tell you: Love your enemies and pray for those who persecute you, that you may be sons of your Father in heaven" (Matthew 5:43-45). And Proverbs 25:21, 22 teaches us, "If your enemy is hungry, give him food to eat; if he is thirsty, give him water to drink … and the LORD will reward you."

Who is your enemy? There are enemies of your country, enemies of God, or dishonest people who seem to "have it out" for you. Kids recognize enemies, too, as bullies on the playground or the tough kid up the block. Kids know what enemies are—but they rarely see the good in loving them!

"I destroy my enemies when I make them my friends."
— Abraham Lincoln

- How does friendship repel hatred?
- Why are these wise words to live by?
- Why is it better to have friends than enemies?

Remind your child that loving our enemies helps us be more like Christ. In fact, Jesus told us to love others as we love ourselves! Ask your child if there is someone with whom he doesn't get along or like. Encourage your child to ask God to bless that person. Ask him to find something nice to do for that individual. Bottom line: Keep praying!

PARENTS POINTER

It's hard to want the best for someone who has humiliated us. Matthew 5:44 says, "Pray for those who persecute you." Encourage your child to pray for the person, whether she feels like it or not. Then let God work on the situation. This method will help your child deal with difficult people in a godly fashion throughout her life.

God calls us to forgive and love our enemies. Help your child understand that it is easy to love the people who love us. But God wants us to love people who may not love us back. Actively pray as a family for enemies or unkind people. Learning to love our enemies builds faith in indescribable and powerful ways!

BIG BIBLE POINT

Proverbs 25:21, 22 speaks of "heaping coals of fire upon his head." Some scholars believe this refers to priests placing coals in censors with incense. They would swing the smoking collection over the heads of the Hebrews to purify and allow them to be closer to God. Loving our enemies can also act like a magnet to draw people to Jesus.

Valuing Others

The more people we introduce our children to, the more comfortable they will feel in any situation. It's important to teach our kids to honor people of varying ages and backgrounds. Their interactions might influence people for Christ, which not only brings glory to God but helps kids become part of the beautiful tapestry of His kingdom!

Give the gift of respect.

One way to honor and influence people is to give them respect. Although respect was at one time an expected rule of behavior for young people, it now often seems to be the exception. Your children can learn to respect the people they meet and hopefully make a lasting impression on them for God.

Respect your superiors.

Respect is honoring others by the kind ways we act toward them. Jesus gave us the best example of respect in the way He placed Himself in a lowly position in order to respect God's will (Philippians 2:5-10). As His followers, we're to humble ourselves for others as well.

RESPECT HONORS OTHERS REGARDLESS OF AGE.

How can we teach our kids to respect others? First of all, we as parents must model it, which means we must check our behavior. Second, we can teach them through practical activities like demonstrating good listening skills. Being a good listener will help your kids understand others better. You can also remind your children to say "Yes, ma'am" and "No, sir" instead of just grunting. That offers a level of respect that honors and influences people.

TARGET MOMENT

Try these ways to show respect for others:

- Say "Yes, sir" and "No, ma'am."
- Compliment family members.
- Call people by name often.
- Find something kind to say.
- Show interest in others!
- Thank others liberally.

Teach your child to respect his siblings. Allowing each child to make a list of simple rules for his own room makes it easier for kids to respect siblings by following the list. Limit the rules to five that can be accomplished, avoiding generalities like "don't breathe on me." The more value a person has in our eyes, the easier it will be to respect him. Encourage your child to find one thing he can like in everyone.

key point

FAMILY MEMBERS DESERVE RESPECT.

key point

WE RESPECT THOSE WE LOOK UP TO.

- How respectful are you of strangers?
- How do you treat your spouse?
- Do you respect your children?
- Do you respect others, like clerks?

"Dear friends, since God so loved us, we also ought to love one another." (1 John 4:11)

Respect your elders.

key point

EMBRACE ELDERLY WISDOM.

Older people were once among the most honored people in our society. In the Bible, being old is an achievement: "Gray hair is a crown of splendor" (Proverbs 16:31). Older folks were the wisest people in the community because wisdom and knowledge came from experience. But somewhere in modern times, the old and wise became elderly and feeble and began to be treated as burdens on society.

You can help your child learn to value the wisdom and experience of older people. If you have grandparents nearby, arrange for your child to spend quality time with them. If they aren't near, consider adopting a set of "grandparents" from your church or neighborhood. Help your kids relate to their elders by encouraging them to ask thought-provoking questions about times when they were younger.

Reach out to the elderly with a hug— and your heart!

TIPS FOR TODDLERS

Even toddlers can say, "Yes, ma'am" and "No, sir" to their elders. They can hold doors open and hold an older person's hand as they walk through the door. Let young children feel the joy in respecting those who are older.

TRY THIS!

Have a living history night! Invite one or two older people for dinner and interview them during the meal. Ask:

- *Where were you born? Where have you lived?*

- *What kind of toys did you have?*

- *What did you do for entertainment as a kid?*

- *What was your school like?*

- *What was it like when there were no computers?*

- *What about World War II?*

Encourage your kids to look for ways to help people, especially the elderly. Hold doors open, patiently carry bags, or return grocery carts for them. Challenge your kids to smile and greet one older person each day to spread smiles. Your kids can find a wealth of wisdom, knowledge, and living history in older people! Help them discover this rewarding resource.

GIFTS KIDS CAN OFFER THEIR ELDERS

ENCOURAGING HUGS

CAREFUL LISTENING

SINCERE QUESTIONS

HELP WITH CHORES

QUALITY TIME

key point
OLDER PEOPLE HAVE LOTS TO OFFER!

Share 1 Peter 2:17 with your child, then discuss the following questions:

- *Why is showing respect a way to honor others?*

- *In what ways can we show "proper" respect?*

- *How does respecting others show God we love and honor Him?*

Respect good sportsmanship.

The great coach Vince Lombardi supposedly said, "Winning isn't everything, it's the only thing." Whether he actually said that is subject to debate, but we often act like winning *is* the only thing. Children's sports, once a place where kids could come together for some fun competition and to learn how to get along with others, are now often places where violence breaks out among the parents. Colleges "buy" promising players for their team with gifts, tutors, and special privileges. Cheating is preferable to losing.

key point
PLAYING FAIR MAKES EVERYONE A WINNER!

What can we do to keep sportsmanship in sports? We must teach our kids what a good sport looks like: one who works hard in practice and in competition but who knows how to lose graciously; one who is a real team player, not a show-off who steals the limelight for himself; one who is respectful to the opposing team. It sounds impossible, but it can be done!

Good sports have more fun!

Think about how you model sportsmanship for your child. Do you ...

• Yell mean things at opposing teams or the TV?

• Make bad comments about the referees?

• Encourage aggressive play in your child?

• React negatively when your team loses?

• Criticize players who didn't perform well?

key point
TREAT OTHERS WITH RESPECT.

You'll never lose when you play fair!

Encourage your child to play hard, but also to play fairly in any game—big or small. Don't allow cheating or throwing tantrums when they lose. Kids must learn that, although playing hard is good and it's fun to win, playing emotionally will cause problems. Teach your children to acknowledge the opposing team or opponent when they play well.

Remind your children that Jesus said, "Do to others as you would have them do to you" (Luke 6:31). At the center of poor sportsmanship is the devaluation of another human being. Being a good sport means not cheating or screaming angrily at the referee. It means bringing grace and integrity to every game. This is what makes your children more than winners—and bright stars who shine Jesus to coaches and teammates!

YOUR CHILD MAY NOT BE ON A SPORTS TEAM, BUT HE WILL WATCH OTHERS COMPETE—AND MIRROR WHAT YOU SAY AND DO. NOW IS THE TIME TO CHEER WISELY AND KINDLY!

Make a special sports award! Let your child design a certificate on the computer to honor family members as they work on sportsmanship. (Have each family member sign the awards and write comments!) Present the framed awards when good sportsmanship is modeled, then throw a pizza party.

key point
MODEL GRACE AND INTEGRITY.

Give the gift of encouragement!

We hunger for encouragement from others. It can brighten our day when we receive it or someone else's day when we give it. Encouragement can even change lives!

Encourage and uplift others.

key point
EVERYONE NEEDS ENCOURAGE-MENT.

key point
BUILD EACH OTHER UP IN CHRIST!

Everyone wants it. We all need it—the gift of encouragement! But it seems like criticism comes out of our mouths much more quickly and easily. The German writer Goethe once said, "Correction does much, but encouragement does more." How often do we, as parents and spouses, encourage those in our family?

TRY THIS!

Place stickers, notepaper, candy, and other items in a bucket. When your child wants to encourage someone, he can prepare a special card and treat. Help your child express encouragement—he might surprise you with encouraging words when you need them most!

The Bible has a lot to say about encouragement. Through God's Word and Paul's letters, we learn that encouragement deflects sin's deceitfulness, gives us hope and endurance, and provides a spirit of unity among us. God gives people encouragement through the Comforter—the Holy Spirit. And God desires us to offer encouragement and help as we draw closer to one another.

> The Greek word for encouragement is *parakeleo*, a verb that means "to call alongside, to uplift or exhort." The idea is that a person will put an arm around a discouraged friend's shoulders and give him a pep talk. The Holy Spirit has a similar name: *Parakletos*, a noun describing someone who is called alongside to give comfort or intercession.

Cheer one another on to good works!

How do we teach our kids to encourage others? Ask them to think of themselves as a Holy Spirit Cheering Squad! The goal is to take notice when someone needs some "cheering on" and then do it. Start in your family by looking for ways to encourage one another. Bake cookies, write notes, or leave a secret encouragement candy bar on someone's pillow.

By practicing with family members, your kids will soon be ready to widen their cheering section. Ask if there is someone at school who might need some cheering on or encouragement. Then brainstorm what could be done. Make being a member of the Holy Spirit Cheering Squad a wonderful habit—for your whole family!

TIPS FOR TODDLERS
Toddlers can give encouraging hugs, and often these are the best encouragement on the planet! If your little ones are willing to be the "official" family huggers, let them!

> "Flatter me, and I may not believe you. Criticize me, and I may not like you. Ignore me, and I may not forgive you. Encourage me, and I will not forget you. Love me, and I may be forced to love you."
>
> **—William Arthur Ward**

Show hospitality to others.

The Bible encourages hospitable activity—making others feel welcomed in our homes. We are encouraged to "not forget to entertain strangers, for by so doing some people have entertained angels without knowing it" (Hebrews 13:2). One of the requirements of an elder is to be hospitable, and we're encouraged to "offer hospitality to one another without grumbling" (1 Peter 4:9).

key point
WELCOME OTHERS WARMLY.

key point
MAKE OTHERS FEEL AT HOME.

Hospitality is an important quality to have, so what's the best way to teach our kids to be more hospitable? Explain that you want to work on welcoming others and showing warm hospitality. Have your child invite a friend over for dinner, snacks, or dessert. Your kids might prefer pizza and a movie or games if several of their friends come.

YOU DON'T HAVE TO SERVE A FOUR-COURSE MEAL TO OFFER HOSPITALITY! A COLD DRINK OR FRESHLY BAKED COOKIES MAKE OTHERS FEEL WARM AND WELCOME IN YOUR HOME.

Hospitality means opening your door—and your heart—to others!

By planning a special get-together once a month and putting it on the calendar, you are more likely to do it. Let the kids help plan the get-together. Assign each child one night to be in charge of hospitality. You'll be the helper, but your kids must organize the event. Also, you can include your children in the preparations of the house. Divide the cleaning chores so everyone takes part.

TARGET MOMENT

As with any virtue, remember to pray with your child about ways to show hospitality to others. Then let God be in control of what happens.

Make friends feel warm and welcome in your home!

TIPS FOR 'TWEENS

Even if your 'tween is shy, there may be someone he would like to have over. Or have a movie marathon with munchies. Remember: You are the assistant. Your 'tween can be the "host with the most!"

TRY THIS!

Make the most of instant get-togethers!

• Keep hot dogs in the freezer. They thaw quickly and grill well.

• Watermelon is an inexpensive and fun treat in summer.

• Buy brownie mix and sprinkle chocolate chips on top before baking.

• Keep spaghetti noodles and cans of sauce on hand.

Hospitality often includes food and festivities to welcome others. Consider buying baskets and filling them with treats for people who move into your neighborhood. Offer to host a kids' Bible study in your home. We make lemon bread in large batches, and when we want to show hospitality, a loaf is brought out. Hospitality takes time and effort, but it blesses not only those who come into your home but your children as well.

Celebrate the gift of community.

One of the wonderful things about being a Christian is having brothers and sisters all over the world. God gave us a huge family to help, love, and care for. When we celebrate community, the world isn't as big and scary as it might seem.

Care for God's church.

The Bible teaches much about caring for each other as part of Christ's body in the church. Paul describes various parts of the body and says that each of us must do what we were made to do in order for the body to work well (Romans 12). We're told that we're united by the oneness of faith, baptism, and God. God's Word emphasizes that Christ is the head of this body and it is He who causes it to grow.

key point
THE CHURCH HAS MANY PARTS.

Kids often wonder how they—such a small part of the whole—can care for their church. One way is to help them find and use their God-given talents to serve the church and those who worship there. They can encourage others, sing in a choir, clean and help organize, or even plant flowers outside. Remind them they're caring for God's church!

key point
SERVE GOD BY SERVING YOUR CHURCH.

What part in God's kingdom do you play? When you feel exuberant and enjoy working for God, your children will notice and want to do the same!

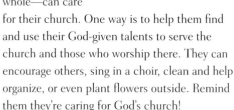

Another interesting thing to do with your kids is to ask them to imagine what it might look like if all of the Christians in the world made up an actual organism. How would this organism get food? How would it grow or move? What might be done to care for this organism? Just thinking "outside of the box" a bit can plant an idea more vividly in your children's minds.

Encourage your kids to participate in church—and in serving God!

61% attended church as kids

PEOPLE WHO PARTICIPATE IN CHURCH TODAY

22% avoided church as kids

(The Barna Group)

Observe your kids to discover what they're naturally good at and the kinds of things they like to do. Match up their interests with ways to serve the church. Try praying for others, cleaning on a Saturday, or passing out hymnals. Encourage your child to serve God and God's family today!

Caring for the body of Christ starts in your own home. How do your children treat each other? How does your family work together? Each member was put in the family for a reason, so brainstorm and discuss what those reasons might be. Not only will it help everyone see how God might be putting you together, but it will also help each person see her spiritual gifts and how they can be used for family, church—and God!

Care for God's world.

Not only are we to care for Christ's body within our families and church, but we can care for each other in our cities and countries around the world. As we express our gratitude at being a part of God's kingdom, it's natural to seek ways to bring hope, compassion, and love to our sisters and brothers in Christ and to others who struggle daily for survival.

key point
WE'RE CITIZENS OF GOD'S WORLD!

"THE LOVE OF ONE'S COUNTRY IS A SPLEN-DID THING. BUT WHY SHOULD LOVE STOP AT THE BORDER?"
—PABLO CASALS

Helping our kids care about their country is fairly easy—just share with them histories of the United States or of your area. You can participate in patriotic events or rent docu-mentaries about your country and its monuments. Have your child help check out local resources that offer patriotic-type activities. And pray for your country and its people!

TARGET MOMENT

If your church supports mis-sionaries, find out all you can about the country they serve. Write notes, pray, and even host a fund-raiser to contribute to the care of the missionary families.

WHY SHOULD WE CARE ABOUT THE WORLD?

- God made and loved the world. (Genesis 2:7)
- God sent His Son to redeem the world. (John 3:16)
- God wants us to teach, preach, and help others the world over. (Matthew 24:14)

Help your child realize we have brothers and sisters all over the globe who welcome our prayers, interest, and help. Discuss current events around the world and explain they touch us because they affect parts of Christ's body. Pick a country to regularly pray for as a family. Look up information from Voice of the Martyrs, an organization that keeps a prayerful eye on people suffering for their faith around the world. This will help your family pray more specifically.

Buy a world map or puzzle of your country. When something happens in the news, let your kids find (and pray for) the place of the event.

Philippians 3:20 reminds us we're citizens in more than one place! Share this verse with your child, then ask:

- *Where are we citizens of?*
- *In what ways are we citizens of heaven?*
- *How can we express our loyalty as citizens of heaven as we would loyalty to a certain country?*

key point
GOOD CITIZENS HELP OTHERS.

Encourage your child to look up places on a map that he has read about in the Bible. Learn about the history of the Christian church, not only in Bible times but also in more modern times. Remind your child that God gave us a big world filled with wonderful people and that through our love for God, we can learn about, help, pray, and care for people everywhere!

Love your country, God, and the world!

More Resources

BOOKS

for parents

- William J. Bennett and Michael Hague, *A Children's Book of Virtues* (Simon & Schuster, 1995).
- Charles Franklin Boyd, David Boehi, and Robert A. Rohom, *Different Children, Different Needs: Understanding the Unique Personality of Your Child* (Multnomah, 2004).
- David Keirsey, *Please Understand Me II: Temperament, Character, Intelligence* (Prometheus Nemesis, 1998).
- Colin Greer and Herbert Kohl, *A Call to Character* (Perennial, 1997).
- Jamie C. Miller, *10-Minute Life Lessons for Kids* (Perennial, 1998).
- Michele Borba, *Building Moral Intelligence: The Seven Essential Virtues That Teach Kids to Do the Right Thing* (Jossey-Bass, 2002).
- Gary D. Chapman and Ross Campbell, *The Five Love Languages of Children* (Moody, 1997).

for kids

- Shel Silverstein, *The Giving Tree* (HarperCollins, 1964). Giving and generosity; ages 3+.
- Virginia Lee Burton, *Mike Mulligan and His Steam Shovel* (Houghton Mifflin, 1939). Faith and perseverance; ages 3-8.

- Lucy Maude Montgomery, *Anne of Green Gables* (Children's Classics, 1998). Honesty and kindness; ages 8+.
- C. S. Lewis, *The Lion, the Witch, and the Wardrobe* (HarperCollins, 1998). Restraint and truth; ages 8+.

VIDEOS AND DVDS

- *"The Call"* (Mars Hill Productions, Houston, Texas.) True story of girl who started Bible clubs throughout her city. Ages 11+.
- George Winston, *The Velveteen Rabbit* (Rabbit Ears Productions, Windham Hill Productions.) An audio CD story about the power of love in making us real! Ages 3+.

WEB SITES

- **www.teachingvalues.com.** Helpful tools and activities for character education.
- **www.charactercounts.org.** Teaching character building.
- **www.gospelcom.net.** Over eighty Christian resource organizations.
- There are a number of really good short-term mission organizations, including Youth With a Mission (ywam.org), Youth for Christ's Project Serve (www.yfc.net), or World Servants (www.worldservants.org).

Subpoint Index

Chapter 3: Valuing Love   52

Chapter 4: Valuing Others   78